Programming for the Beginner

by

Tobias Amdahl

Revised 2016/11/30

Contents

III   Conclusion   100

Part I

Getting Started

Programming and Programming Languages

A "program" is a set of instructions that tells a computer how to do something. Programs can be "run", or "executed", to make a computer do useful or entertaining things.

A "programming language" is a language that a program's instructions are written in. This book will teach you how to make programs using a programming language called "JavaScript".

This book assumes that your computer is running either Microsoft Windows or a Linux-based operating system that runs the Gnome2 or Cinnamon desktop environment, and that it has a web browser that can run JavaScript installed on it. And even if your computer runs some other operating system, as long as it has a good web browser, it should still be possible to run the programs in this book, with some minor tweaks.

Getting Ready to Program

Follow the steps below to get your computer ready to start creating programs.

1. Start the computer and wait for the computer to "boot". Eventually, a "login" screen will appear.

2. On the login screen, enter the correct username and password in the boxes. If you don't know a username and password that works, ask whoever owns the computer.

3. After entering the username and password, move the mouse pointer over the login button (which might look like an arrow pointing right), then press and quickly release the left mouse button. This is called "clicking" the button. When the login button is clicked, the computer will finish starting up, and eventually the main screen will appear. The main screen in a operating system with a graphical user interface is called the "desktop".

4. Move the mouse pointer over an empty space on the desktop and click the right button. This is called "right-clicking", while clicking the left mouse button is just called "clicking". When the desktop is right-clicked, a list of options, called a "menu", will appear. This particular kind of menu is called a "context menu".

5a. If your computer is running Microsoft Windows, move the mouse pointer until it is located over the item "New" in the context menu. Then let the mouse stay still for a moment, which is called "hovering". When you hover over the "New" item, another menu, which we'll call a "submenu", will appear next to the first menu. In the submenu, move the mouse pointer over the "Folder" item and click it.

5b. If you computer is running a Linux-based operating system, move the mouse pointer over the item "Create Folder" and click it.

6. A picture of a folder will appear on the desktop, and some placeholder text like "New folder" Or "untitled folder" will appear below

it. The picture is called an "icon", and the text below the icon is the name of the new folder. When the folder is first created, its name will be highlighted. While the name of the new folder is highlighted, use the keyboard to type the word "Programs" (without the quotes) and press the Enter key. The new folder will be renamed "Programs".

8. Move the mouse-pointer over icon of the Programs folder and click the mouse button twice rapidly. This is called a "double-click". Double-clicking the folder's icon will cause a window to appear that shows the items contained in the folder. Right now, the Programs folder is empty, so no items will appear.

9. Right-click on an empty spot in the background of the Programs folder window. Another context menu will appear.

10a. If your computer is running Microsoft Windows, hover over the "New" menu item, and then click the "Text Document" item in the submenu. A new icon will appear, with the name "New Text Document.txt" below it. If the name reads "New Text Document" with no ".txt" after it, it means that Windows is set to hide this information, called a "file extension", from the user. This setting must be changed in order to use the lessons in this book. To change this setting, first, press the "Alt" key. A menu bar will appear at the top of the folder window. Press the "T" key to display the contents of the "Tools" menu, then press the "O" key to open a new window named "Folder Options". Click on the "View" tab at the top of this window. On the View tab, locate the "Advanced settings" pane, and locate the checkbox labeled "Hide extensions for known file types" within that pane. Click the checkbox to deactivate it, then click the OK button to confirm the change and dismiss the Folder Options window. Back in the folder window, the name of the newly created file should now end with ".txt".

10b. If your computer is running a Linux-based operating system, hover over the "Create Document" item and then click the "Empty File" item in the submenu. A new icon will appear, with the name "new file" below it.

11. Just like with the folder created earlier, the name of the new file will initially be highlighted. Type the name "Setup.html" and press the Enter key to change the name.

12. Right-click the icon of the file Setup.html. Another context menu will appear.

13a. If your computer is running Microsoft Windows, hover over the "Open With" item in the context menu, and click the "Choose default program..." item from the submenu. A "dialog box" will appear, with the name "Open with" across the top. On the "Open with" dialog, locate the icon for the text editor program "Notepad", which should look like an actual notepad, and double-click it. The dialog will "be dismissed", which means it disappears, and the file "Setup.html" will be "opened" in Notepad, which means you can add and change the text in it. In fact, now whenever you double-click a file whose name ends with ".html", it will be opened with the Notepad text editor.

13b. If your computer is running a Linux-based operating system, hover over the "Open With" item in the context menu, and click the "Other Application..." item from the submenu. A "dialog box" will appear, with the name "Open With" across the top. On the "Open With" dialog, locate the icon for the text editor program "gedit" (pronounced "gee edit"), which should look like an physical notepad, and double-click it. The dialog will be dismissed, and the file "Setup.html" will be "opened" in gedit, which means you can add and change the text in it. In fact, now whenever you double-click a file whose name ends with ".html", it will be opened with the gedit text editor.

14. Click the text editor window and type the text that appears between the horizontal lines below into it, exactly as it appears. To indent the lines that need indenting, you can either press the space bar several times or just press the Tab key once. On most keyboards, the Tab key is just to the left of the Q key.

```
<html>
<body>
        <p>This isn't really a program.</p>
        <p>It's just a web page.</p>
        <p>JavaScript programs are often found in web pages.</p>
</body>
</html>
```

15. Near the top of the text editor window, just underneath the title bar, there is the "main menu" bar. When the items on this menu bar are clicked, menus appear underneath them. Click the "File" item on the main menu bar, then click the "Save" item on the menu that appears beneath it. This will cause the changes you made to "Setup.html" to be written back to the file.

16. Open a web browser (such as Mozilla Firefox or Google Chrome) and wait for the web browser window to appear.

17. In the window for the Programs folder, move the mouse pointer over the icon for "Setup.html", then hold down the left mouse button. With the left mouse button held down, move the mouse pointer over the web browser window and let go of the mouse button. This is called a "drag and drop". It will cause Setup.html to be opened in the web browser, and a web page will be displayed.

18. If everything appears normal, "close" the text editor window in which Setup.html is being edited, perhaps by clicking the "X" button in its upper right-hand corner.

Part II

Programs

Comments

The program on the next page does nothing, because it is made up entirely of "comments".

Comments don't do anything, but they let the programmer make notes that might help anyone reading the program to understand it more easily.

Create a new text file named "Comments.html" in the Programs folder, open it in a text editor, enter the text on the next page into it, save it, and drag the file onto a web browser window to run it.

```
<html>
<body>
<p>There's a program on this page, but it doesn't do anything!</p>
<script type="text/javascript">

        // This is technically a program,
        // but it doesn't do anything.

        // Everything on a line
        // that comes after the symbol "//"
        // is called a "comment".

        /* Anything between these symbols is also a comment . */
        /*
                Even if it takes up
                more than one line.
        */

</script>
</body>
</html>
```

Hello, World

The program on the next page, when run, displays the message "Hello, world!".

There is only one line in the program, which is:

```
alert("Hello, world!");
```

This line is called a "statement".

The message "Hello, world!" is an example of a "string". A string is a piece of text. In JavaScript, a string is created by putting text between a pair of double-quotes (").

Create a new text file named "HelloWorld.html" in the Programs folder, open it in a text editor, enter the text on the next page into it, save it, and drag the file onto a web browser window to run it.

```
<html>
<body>
<script type="text/javascript">

        alert("Hello, world!");

</script>
</body>
</html>
```

Debugging

Now that we've written a program that runs correctly, it's time to talk about what to do when a program is written incorrectly. When a program is written incorrectly, it may not do what the programmer expects it to do. Often it may not do anything at all.

Programmers often make mistakes. Mistakes in a program are called "errors", or "bugs". Figuring out why these errors are happening and fixing them is called "debugging".

The program between the horizontal lines below is written incorrectly on purpose, in order to show how debugging works.

```
<html>
<body>
<script type="text/javascript">

        // The closing quote is missing
        // on the string "Hello, world!".
        // This is an error.

        alert("Hello, world!);

</script>
</body>
</html>
```

Follow the steps given in previous sections to create the program, but this time name the file "Debugging.html". Drag the file's icon onto a web browser window to run it. (Most modern web browsers provide some way to debug JavaScript programs, but in this book, we're assuming that the web browser is being used is either Mozilla Firefox or Google Chrome.)

No message will appear when the program is run, because there is an error in it. To start debugging, press the F12 key. A debugging pane will appear at the bottom of the web browser window. (If it doesn't, it may be because your computer is configured so that the F1-F12 keys do things like adjusting the brightness of the monitor or the volume of the speakers. In that case, look for a key named "Fn" or "F-Lock" and try pressing it or holding it down before pressing F12.)

Click the tab named "Console". The Console pane will appear. In the Console pane, some text describing the error should be visible. If Firefox is being used, the error message might be:

`SyntaxError: unterminated string literal`

In Google Chrome, the error message might be:

`Uncaught SyntaxError: Invalid or unexpected token`

Either of these error messages means that the programmer forgot to put a closing quote at the end of a string.

To the right of the error message is a link that names the file the error occurred in ("Debugging.html") and the line number it occurred on. Click this link. Another window will appear, showing the program, with a highlight on the line that caused the error.

Back in the text editor, fix the code by adding a double-quote to the end of the string, save it, and refresh the web page. The message "Hello, world!" will appear.

Variables

The next program also displays "Hello, world!", but it uses a "variable" to do it.

Variables are used to store pieces of information, called "data". This program stores the string "Hello, world!" in a variable named "message", and then displays it.

A variable is "declared" using the "var" keyword, followed by the name of the variable. A variable declaration looks like this:

```
var message;
```

Once a variable has been declared, data can be stored in it. The data stored in a variable is called its "value". A variable's value is set or changed using an "assignment statement", which uses the assignment "operator" ("="), and looks like this:

```
message = "Hello, world!";
```

The "=" operator is pronounced "gets", so this assignment statement would be pronounced "message gets hello world".

Assigning a value to a variable for the first time is called "initializing" that variable. A variable can be declared and initialized on a single line, which would look like this:

```
var message = "Hello, world!";
```

Declaring a variable can be imagined as taking a folder and writing the variable's name it. The variable can then be set by writing the desired value on a piece of paper, putting the paper inside the folder, and setting the folder aside for later use. When it is needed, the value stored in a variable can be retrieved and used by finding the folder with the right name on it and reading the piece of paper inside. You could also change the value stored in a variable by simply taking out the old piece of paper and putting in a new one, with a different value written on it.

Follow the steps given in previous sections to create and run the program below.

```html
<html>
<body>
<script type="text/javascript">

        // Declare the variable.
        var message;

        // Assign a string value to the variable.
        message = "Hello, world!";

        // Display the message.
        alert(message);

</script>
</body>
</html>
```

String Concatenation

The next program greets a person by name.

The program uses the symbol "+", which is an example of an operator, to join multiple strings together into a longer string. Joining strings in this way is called "concatenation".

Follow the steps given in previous sections to create and run the program.

```
<html>
<body>
<script type="text/javascript">

        // Declare and assign a variable.
        var personName = "Joe";

        // Build a message using the variable.
        var message = "Hello, " + personName + "!";

        // Display the message.
        alert(message);

</script>
</body>
</html>
```

Variable Names

The name of a variable is also called an "identifier".

Only certain symbols are allowed in an identifier. An identifier must start with a letter or an underscore (" _"), and can contain no spaces, and no symbols other than letters, numbers, and underscores. Furthermore, it can't be the same as a JavaScript "keyword". A keyword is a word that the programming language reserves for its own use, like "var".

Some examples of valid and invalid variable names are given on the next page.

Many beginning programmers give their variables very short names, maybe even a single letter. While names this short may be appropriate some of the time, often they make it harder to read and understand the program. In these cases, it is better to make the variable name a little longer. In general, variable names should be long and descriptive enough to make their meaning clear, without having to spend time figuring out what some abbreviation is supposed to stand for.

Another way to make variable names easier to read is to use "camel-case". Camel-case is the practice of capitalizing the first letter in each "word" in the variable name. For example, the camel-cased version of the variable name "numberoffishinthesea" would be "numberOfFishInTheSea". The camel-cased version is much more readable.

The program on the next page shows some valid and invalid names for variable names. Some lines are "commented out", which means that they are turned into comments by adding the comment symbol "//" in front of them. Commenting out these lines means that they won't cause errors when the program is run.

```
<html>
<body>
<script type="text/javascript">

        // Some valid variable names.

        var validName = "value"; // This is okay.
        var _validName = "value"; // So is this.
        var VALID_NAME = "value"; // And this.
        var validName123 = "value"; // This too.

        // Some invalid variable names.
        // If these weren't "commented out",
        // they would prevent the program from running.

        // var 1invalidName = "value"; // This is not okay.
        // var invalid name = "value"; // Neither is this.
        // var INVALID-NAME = "value"; // Nor this.
        // var isThisNameValid? = false; // Nor this.
        // var !@#$%^&* = "???"; // This neither.
        // var var = "value"; // This is not okay.

</script>
</body>
</html>
```

Variable Names and Capitalization

In a variable name, it matters which letters are uppercase and which are lowercase.

The next program declares four different variables, called "person-Name", "personname", "PersonName", and "PERSONNAME", and initializes each of them to a different value. It then displays the values of each of these variables.

The purpose of this program is to show that, in order to access the value of a variable, you must write the name of the variable in exactly the same way that it was declared. Changing even a single letter means accessing a completely different variable.

Follow the steps given in previous sections to create and run the program.

```
<html>
<body>
<script type="text/javascript">

        // All of these are different variables,
        // because case is significant.
        var personName = "Robert";
        var personname = "Bobby";
        var PersonName = "Rob";
        var PERSONNAME = "Bob";

        // Display the value of each variable.
        alert("personName is " + personName);
        alert("personname is " + personname);
        alert("PersonName is " + PersonName);
        alert("PERSONNAME is " + PERSONNAME);

</script>
</body>
</html>
```

Debugging with Breakpoints and Watches

In a previous section, the JavaScript debugger built into the web browser was used to locate an error in a program that prevented it from running. The debugger has many other features. With "breakpoints" and "watches", the programmer can pause the execution of the program on any line, "step through" the statements in the program line by line, and track any changes to the values assigned to variables as the program runs.

To get started, follow the steps given in previous sections to create and run the program between the horizontal lines below.

```
<html>
<body>
<script type="text/javascript">

        // Set a "breakpoint" on the line below.
        var personName = "Archie";
        alert("Hello, " + personName + "!");

        var personName = "Beth";
        alert("Hello, " + personName + "!");

        var personName = "Charlie";
        alert("Hello, " + personName + "!");

        var personName = "Dave";
        alert("Hello, " + personName + "!");

        alert("Hello, everybody!");

</script>
</body>
</html>
```

As the program runs, click the OK button on each of the dialogs that appear to dismiss them one by one.

22

In the web browser window, bring up the debugging pane, perhaps by pressing the F12 key.

If using Google Chrome, locate the "Watch" tab in the debugging pane and click it, then click the "+" icon within the Watch pane.

If using Mozilla Firefox, click the "Debugger" tab, click the "Expand Panes" icon within the Debugger pane, click the "Variables" tab within the pane that appears, click the "Add watch expression" link within the Variables pane.

At the prompt, enter the value "personName" Make sure that the capitalization is correct, then press the Enter key. This will create a new "watch" on the personName variable. The current value of the personName will appear in this area, and will be updated whenever the value of the variable changes.

If using Google Chrome, click the "Sources" tab at the top of the debugging pane, then click the "Show Navigator" icon on the toolbar that appears below it. In the pane that appears to the left, click the Sources tab, then locate the name of the program's .html file within the tree view and click it.

Locate the code listing for the program and click the line number to the left of the first line of the program, the one that sets the value of the personName variable to "Archie". An indicator of some sort (for example, a dot or an arrow) will appear next to the line number, indicating that a "breakpoint" has been set on the line.

Click the Refresh button or press the F5 key to re-start the program. The program will start, and execution will be paused at the first line in the program. In the "Watch" pane, the value of the personName variable will be shown to be "undefined".

Press the F10 key to "step over" to the next line of code. (You could also do this by clicking the appropriate button in one of the debugging pane's toolbars, currently rendered in both Chrome and Firefox as a curved arrow arching over a dot.) The initial assignment of the personName variable will be performed, and the Watch pane will automatically be updated to show the variable's new value "Archie".

Press the F10 key again. A dialog saying "Hello, Archie!" will appear. Click the OK button on this dialog to dismiss it. The program will execute the next two lines of code, and the value of the personName variable in the Watch pane will change to "Beth".

Locate the Console pane. If using Google Chrome, it may be visible at the bottom of the debugging pane. If using Mozilla Firefox, you'll need to click the "Console" tab at the top of the debugging pane.

Click on the Console pane, type the text "personName + personName" at the prompt, and press the Enter key. You should see the text "BethBeth" appear in the console. This shows that you can enter arbitrary expressions in the console window and have them evaluated immediately.

If using Mozilla Firefox, click on the Debugger tab to switch back to the code listing again.

Press the F8 key (or click the appropriate button in the toolbar, currently a right-pointing triangle in both Chrome and Firefox) to resume execution of the program. Dismiss all the dialogs as necessary until the program completes.

(This page intentionally left blank to preserve section format.)

Data Types

The next program shows several variables being assigned values of three different "data types".

Variables in JavaScript can contain values of many different types. The value of a variable may be a string, a number, or a "boolean", which is a true-or-false, yes-or-no value.

Variables can also contain more complex values, like a mailing address, or a recipe for pie, a list of other variables, or even a whole other program! This will be described in more detail later.

The program also makes use of the "+" symbol, which in this case is used to combine two strings into a larger one. This symbol will be described in more detail in the next section.

Follow the steps given in previous sections to create and run the program.

```
<html>
<body>
<script type="text/javascript">

        // Assign values of various data types to variables.
        var one = 1; // An integer (whole) number.
        var pi = 3.14; // A "floating-point" number.
        var lameCatchPhrase = "You got it, dude!"; // A string.
        var isThePopeCatholic = true; // A "boolean".
        var isBreadLoCarb = false; // Another boolean.

        // Display the variables' values.
        // All these values
        // are automatically converted to strings
        // by the concatenation operator ("+").
        alert("one is " + one);
        alert("pi is " + pi);
        alert("lameCatchPhrase is " + lameCatchPhrase);
        alert("isThePopeCatholic is " + isThePopeCatholic);
        alert("isBreadLoCarb is " + isBreadLoCarb);

</script>
</body>
</html>
```

Operators and Expressions

The next program stores two numbers in two variables, finds their sum, stores that sum in a third variable, builds a text string from those variables, stores that string in yet another variable, and finally displays that string.

The program uses the symbol "+" in several places. The "+" symbol is an example of an "operator". An operator is used to perform an "operation" on one or more values in JavaScript. The values used in a particular operation are called "operands". A set of operators and the operands they operate on is called an "expression".

Operators and operands are used in basic arithmetic. In the equation "$1 + 2 = 3$", the operator is "+", the operation is "addition", and the operands are 1 and 2.

In JavaScript, the "+" operator can work in much the same way as in mathematics. If the operands of the "+" operator are variables whose values are numbers, it will add them together and calculate their sum. The result of this expression can then be stored in another variable.

When the operands of the "+" operator are strings rather than numbers, the operator "concatenates" them into a longer string. The result of this expression is the contents of the first string followed by the contents of the second.

If one of the operands is a number and the other is a string, the number is automatically converted to a string before concatenation. For example, in the program on the next page, there is a variable named "augend", whose value is the number 1, which is automatically converted to the string "1" before concatenation.

Follow the steps given in previous sections to run the program.

```
<html>
<body>
<script type="text/javascript">

        // The values to be added together.
        var augend = 1;
        var addend = 2;

        // Add the variables together.
        var sum = augend + addend;

        // Build a message string from augend, addend, and sum.
        var message = augend + " + " + addend + " = " + sum;

        // Display the message.
        alert(message);

</script>
</body>
</html>
```

DOM Elements

The next program, like the one in a previous section, greets a person by name, but instead of calling the "alert()" function, it creates a "DOM" element to contain the message, and "appends" that DOM element to the web page to display it. Since this method doesn't pop up a dialog that needs to be dismissed, it's a somewhat less annoying way to display a message.

"DOM" stands for "Document Object Model". Examples of "DOM objects" include buttons, text boxes, select boxes, headings, blocks of text, images, and other things that might appear on web pages. These things are sometimes also called "controls".

In this program, the DOM object is a "p" element, which represents a "paragraph" of text. This element is stored in a variable named "pGreeting". The contents of the p element are set by this line:

```
pGreeting.innerHTML = message;
```

Follow the steps given in previous sections to create and run the program.

```
<html>
<body>
<script type="text/javascript">

        // Assign the personName variable the string "Joe".
        var personName = "Joe";

        // Build a greeting message.
        var message = "Hello, " + personName + "!";

        // Create a new "p" (paragraph) element.
        var pGreeting = document.createElement("p");

        // Set the contents of the p element to the message.
        pGreeting.innerHTML = message;

        // Attach the p element to the web page,
        // which will cause it to be displayed.
        document.body.appendChild(pGreeting);

</script>
</body>
</html>
```

If And Else Statements

The next program uses "if" and "else" statements to determine which messages will be displayed.

An "if" statement is declared by using the keyword "if" followed by a condition in parentheses, followed by a code block. A "code block", or simply "block", is any set of statements contained within the "" and "" characters, which are called "braces". If the condition is true, the statements inside the block will run. If not, these statements will be skipped.

An if block may (or may not) be immediately followed by an "else" block. The statements inside the else block will only be executed if the if condition is false.

The conditions for the if statements in this program look like this:

```
(isTheSkyBlue == true)
```

These conditions contain the "==" symbol, which is made up of two equals signs. It is pronounced "equals". It is very important not to confuse this with the "=" symbol used in assignment statements, which is pronounced "gets".

Follow the steps given in previous sections to create and run the program. Then try changing the value assigned to the "isTheSkyBlue" variable on the first line of the program to "false", and run the program again to see what happens.

```html
<html>
<body>
<script type="text/javascript">

        // Declare and assign a boolean variable.
        var isTheSkyBlue = true;

        // Check the value of the variable.
        if (isTheSkyBlue == true)
        {
                // Since the variable's value is true,
                // this block will be run,
                // and this message will be displayed.
                alert("The sky is blue.");
        }
        else
        {
                // This block would only run
                // if variable's value were false.

                alert("The sky is NOT blue.");
        }

        // Check the variable again.
        if (isTheSkyBlue == true)
        {
                alert("The sky is STILL blue.");
        }

</script>
</body>
</html>
```

If-Else Chains

The next program uses a "chain" of if and else statements to decide which of several messages to display.

An "else" keyword that appears after an "if" block may be immediately followed by a second "if" block. If this second "if" block is also followed by an "else" keyword, then a third "if" block can be added after the second "else" keyword, and so on.

Follow the steps given in previous sections to create and run the program. Then try changing the value assigned to the "skyColor" variable on the first line of the program and run the program again to see what happens.

```html
<html>
<body>
<script type="text/javascript">

        // Set a variable.
        var skyColor = "blue";

        // Display a message.
        alert("The sky is " + skyColor + "...");

        // Check the variable's actual value
        // against several possible values,
        // and display the approriate message.
        if (skyColor == "black")
        {
                alert("Must be nighttime!");
        }
        else if (skyColor == "red")
        {
                alert("Must be sunrise or sunset!");
        }
        else if (skyColor == "gray")
        {
                alert("It's kind of cloudy today.");
        }
        else if (skyColor == "blue")
        {
                alert("It's a beautiful clear day!");
        }
        else
        {
                // If none of the conditions above were true,
                // this block will be run.
                alert("What does a " + skyColor + " sky mean?");
        }

</script>
</body>
</html>
```

While Loops

The next program displays the same message five times in a row. To do this, it uses a "while loop".

A while loop is declared using the keyword "while", followed by a "loop condition" in parentheses, followed by a block of code contained in braces. The while loop runs the statements inside its braces until the loop condition is no longer true.

Follow the steps given in previous sections to create and run the program.

```html
<html>
<body>
<script type="text/javascript">

        // Display a message five times,
        // using a while loop.
        var i = 0;
        while (i < 5)
        {
                alert("Is this getting annoying yet?");
                i = i + 1;
        }

</script>
</body>
</html>
```

For Loops

The next program does almost the same thing as the preceding one, but instead of a while loop, it uses a "for" loop.

A for loop is declared by using the keyword "for", followed by a set of parentheses containing an initialization statement, a loop condition, and a "step" statement, separated by semicolons.

A for loop is basically just a more compact method of writing a while loop. But because the programmer must put the initialization and step statements in the same set of parentheses with the loop condition, a for loop makes the program easier to understand when reading it, and makes it harder to make a mistake when writing it. Compare the while loop in the previous program to the for loop in this one.

Follow the steps given in previous sections to create and run the program.

```
<html>
<body>
<script type="text/javascript">

        // Display a message five times,
        // this time using a for loop.
        for (var i = 0; i < 5; i = i + 1)
        {
                alert("Hey! Listen!");
        }

</script>
</body>
</html>
```

Arrays

The next program displays a list of numbers, from zero to three. It stores the names of these numbers not in four different variables, but rather in a single "array".

An "array" is a variable that contains not a single value but rather a list of values. These values are called the "elements" of the array. Normally, all of the elements in an array are of the same data type. Foor example, an array might contain all strings or all numbers.

Each array element has an "index", which is the item's position in the array. The first element in an array has an index of 0, which is often surprising to the beginning programmer. The second item's index is 1, the third's is 2, and so on.

An array can be assigned by putting the desired element values between the "[" and "]" characters. For example, an array named "planetsBySize" that contains the names of all the planets of the solar system in descending order of size could be declared and assigned like this:

```
var planetsBySize =
[
        "Jupiter", "Saturn", "Uranus",
        "Neptune", "Earth", "Venus",
        "Mars", "Mercury", "Pluto"
];
```

Once an array has been initialized, the number of items in an array can be accessed by appending the text ".length" to the array's name, like this:

```
var numberOfPlanets = planetsBySize.length;
```

A particular element within an array can be accessed by putting that element's index into square brackets (" []"), and adding that after the array's name. For example, the first, second, and final elements of the planetsBySize array could be accessed like this:

```
var jupiter = planetsBySize[0];
var saturn = planetsBySize[1];
var pluto = planetsBySize[planetsBySize.length - 1];
```

Make a special note of the fact that the index of the last element in an array is one less than the array's length. This is a common cause of errors for beginners.

Finally, if the index of a particular element within an array is not known, it can be accessed by calling the "indexOf()" function of that array with the element's value between the parentheses, like this:

```
var earthsSizeRanking = planetsBySize.indexOf("Earth");
```

Follow the steps given in previous sections to create and run the program. Note that the last statement in the for block's header is "i++", which is just a shorter way of writing "i = i + 1".

```html
<html>
<body>
<script type="text/javascript">

        // Build an array, and assign it to a variable.
        var namesOfNumbers = ["Zero", "One", "Two", "Three"];

        // Determine the number of elements in the array.
        var numberOfNumbers = namesOfNumbers.length;

        // Display each element in the array.
        for (var i = 0; i < numberOfNumbers; i++)
        {
                var numberName = namesOfNumbers[i];
                alert(numberName);
        }

</script>
</body>
</html>
```

(This page intentionally left blank to preserve section format.)

Adding and Removing Array Items

The next program creates an array of colors, adds a color to the end of it, removes an element from it (because it's not a color), inserts another color into it, and then displays the list.

As mentioned in the previous section, you can find the index of an element within an array by calling the "indexOf" function on that array and passing in the item as a parameter. If the item is not present in the array, the value of indexOf() will be -1.

Elements can be added to the end of an array by calling the "push" function on that array and passing in the element to be added as a parameter.

Elements can be removed or inserted into the middle of an array by calling the "splice()" function, which is unfortunately rather more complicated. Study the splice() calls in the program on the next page carefully to see how it works.

Also, note how some of the statements in the program take up more than one line. This was done because the statements were too long to fit on a single line. It is perfectly acceptable to break up a long statement into multiple lines in JavaScript. In general, JavaScript ignores "non-printing" characters like spaces and "newlines" (that is, the character that is "typed" when the enter key is pressed), except of course within string values.

Follow the steps given in previous sections to create and run the program.

```
<html>
<body>
<script type="text/javascript">

        // Build the array.
        var rainbowColors =
        [
                "Red", "Orange", "Green", "Intolerance", "Blue"
        ];

        rainbowColors.push("Violet"); // Add element at end.

        // Remove an element from the array.
        var indexToRemoveAt = rainbowColors.indexOf("Intolerance");
        var numberOfItemsToRemove = 1;
        rainbowColors.splice
        (
                indexToRemoveAt, numberOfItemsToRemove
        );

        var indexToInsertAt = rainbowColors.indexOf("Green");
        numberOfItemsToRemove = 0;
        var itemToInsert = "Yellow";
        rainbowColors.splice
        (
                indexToInsertAt,
                numberOfItemsToRemove,
                itemToInsert
        ); // Insert elements between existing elements.

        // Display all elements in the array.
        for (var i = 0; i < rainbowColors.length; i++)
        {
                alert(rainbowColors[i]);
        }

</script>
</body>
</html>
```

Breaking out of a Loop

Breaking out of a loop is done when the loop has "done its work" and no longer needs to run.

The program on the next page contains a for loop that loops through each element of an array of strings and sees if it is equal to "a delicious seabass". When it finds the "fish" element, a "break" statement is executed, exiting the loop.

Follow the steps given in previous sections to create and run the program.

```html
<html>
<body>
<script type="text/javascript">

        var thingsInTheWater =
        [
                "some seaweed", "a boot", "a merman",
                "my own thumb", "a delicious seabass",
                "a pirate ghost", "malaria", "the other boot",
                "Cthulhu"
        ];

        var thingDesired = "a delicious seabass";

        for (var i = 0; i < thingsInTheWater.length; i++)
        {
                var thingCaught = thingsInTheWater[i];

                alert("I just caught " + thingCaught + "...");

                if (thingCaught == thingDesired)
                {
                        alert("...so I'm going home to eat it.");

                        // We found what we were looking for,
                        // so exit the loop immediately.
                        break;
                }

                alert("...so I'll keep fishing.");
        }

</script>
</body>
</html>
```

Hashtables

JavaScript can also be used to create "hashtables".

A hashtable works sort of like a telephone directory, which allows you to look up the phone number of someone if you know their name, or like the index of a textbook, which allows you to look up the page on which where a particular term appears, or like a dictionary, which allows you to look up the meaning of a word if you know its spelling.

The next program intializes a small telephone directory, adds another name and number to it, then looks up and displays a phone number from it.

In other programming languages, hashtables may be called "lookups", "dictionaries", or "associative arrays". However, it should be noted that even though hashtables are somtimes called "associative arrays", they are still in fact very different from ordinary arrays.

Follow the steps given in previous sections to create and run the program.

```
<html>
<body>
<script type="text/javascript">

        // Create a lookup.
        var nameToPhoneNumberLookup =
        {
                "Angela" : "555-1234",
                "Bob" : "555-5678",
                "Carol" : "555-9012"
        };

        // Add an entry to the lookup.
        nameToPhoneNumberLookup["Joe"] = "555-3456";

        // Find Carol's number in the lookup.
        var personToCall = "Carol";
        var numberToCall = nameToPhoneNumberLookup[personToCall];

        // Display the person's number.
        var message =
                personToCall
                + "'s phone number is "
                + numberToCall
                + ".";

        alert(message);

</script>
</body>
</html>
```

Declaring and Calling a Function

Just like the last program, the next program also greets a person by name, but it declares and calls a "function" to do it.

The function's name is "greetJoe".

The function's "declaration" starts with the line "function greetJoe()". This line is called the function's "header".

The function's "body" is contained in a code block that appears below its header, between the symbols "{" and "}", which are called "curly braces" or just "braces".

On the last line of the program, a "call" is made to the function named "greetJoe". The function call looks like this: "greetJoe();".

Functions can be thought of as smaller programs inside another program. Functions are useful because they reduce the amount of repetition in a program. For example, suppose that a program needs to perform a certain task, and it takes twenty lines of code to do it. Now suppose that the task needs to be performed five times, at various places in the program. Without functions, that would be a hundred lines of code! If those twenty lines of code were moved inside a function, then each of those "extra" sets of twenty lines can be replaced with a single-line function call.

Many of the preceding programs contain calls to "alert()", which is also a function. The alert() function is not, however, declared inside these programs. It is built into JavaScript.

In other programming languages, functions might be called "methods", "procedures", or "subroutines".

Follow the steps given in previous sections to create and run the program.

```html
<html>
<body>
<script type="text/javascript">

        // The "greetJoe()" function's declaration
        // begins on the next line.
        function greetJoe() // This line is the header.
        {
                // Inside the braces is the function's body.
                var personName = "Joe";
                var message = "Hello, " + personName + "!";
                alert(message);
        }
        // The greetJoe() function's declaration ends here.

        // Functions aren't run until they are "called",
        // so greetJoe() hasn't run yet.

        // "Call" the greetJoe() function to run it.
        greetJoe();

</script>
</body>
</html>
```

Function Calls with Arguments

The next program does almost the same thing as the previous one, except that it declares a function that accepts an "argument".

Arguments can be declared in a function's header, between the parentheses. In the program on the next page, the "greetPerson()" function accepts a single argument, which is named "personName".

When the greetPerson() function is called on the last line of the program, a value for this argument must be "passed" into the function by placing a variable name or an expression between the parentheses. Then, within the body of the greetPerson() function, "personName" can be used like a variable to access whatever value was passed into the function.

Passing arguments to functions is a way to make those functions more versatile, and therefore more useful. For example, in the program on the next page, greeting messages for three different people can be displayed simply by changing the value of the argument that is passed to the function.

In some other programming languages, arguments are called "parameters".

Follow the steps given in previous sections to create and run the program.

```
<html>
<body>
<script type="text/javascript">

        // The greetPerson() function
        // takes one "argument", named "personName".
        function greetPerson(personName)
        {
                // Within the function body,
                // the argument can be used as a variable.
                var message = "Hello, " + personName + "!";
                alert(message);
        }

        // Call greetPerson() three times,
        // passing three different arguments,
        // to display three different (but similar) greetings.
        greetPerson("Joe");
        greetPerson("Katherine");
        greetPerson("Luis");

</script>
</body>
</html>
```

Functions with Return Values

When some functions are called, they "return" a value. If a function returns a value, calls to that function can be used as expressions.

The next program declares a function named "add", which adds together the two parameters that are passed to it and returns their sum to the block of code that calls the function. This sum can then be stored in a variable. This is done by using an assignment statement with the function call on its right side, like this:

```
var sum = add(augend, addend);
```

To return a value from a function, the keyword "return" is used, followed by the value to be returned. Any statements that come after a return statement will not be run. For this reason, the return statement, if present, is often the last line in a function.

Other times, a return statement is used to exit from a function early in cases where running the rest of the function is unnecessary. Some programmers prefer not to do this, however, because it can make a program harder to understand.

Follow the steps given in previous sections to create and run the program.

```html
<html>
<body>
<script type="text/javascript">

        // The add() function
        // takes two arguments and returns a value.
        function add(augend, addend)
        {
                // Add the arguments together;
                var sum = augend + addend;
                // Return their sum.
                return sum;
        }

        // Call the add() function
        // and pass in the arguments 3 and 4.
        var augend = 3;
        var addend = 4;
        var sum = add(augend, addend);

        // Display the result.
        alert(augend + " + " + addend + " = " + sum);

        // Call the add() function again,
        // but this time pass in the arguments 5 and 6,
        // without assigning any variables.
        alert("5 + 6 = " + add(5, 6));

</script>
</body>
</html>
```

Nested Function Calls

The next program declares not one but two functions, one of which calls the other. The "greetPerson()" function is called from within the "greetJoe()" function, which is itself called from the last line of the program.

Functions frequently call other functions in JavaScript. Sometimes, functions even call themselves!

Follow the steps given in previous sections to create and run the program.

```
<html>
<body>
<script type="text/javascript">

        // Declare the greetJoe() function.
        function greetJoe()
        {
                // Call the greetPerson() function
                // and pass in "Joe" as the argument.
                greetPerson("Joe");
        }

        // Declare the greetPerson() function.
        function greetPerson(personName)
        {
                var message = "Hello, " + personName + "!";

                // Create p element, set its content, add to page.
                var pGreeting = document.createElement("p");
                pGreeting.innerHTML = message;
                document.body.appendChild(pGreeting);
        }

        // Call the greetJoe() function.
        greetJoe();

</script>
</body>
</html>
```

Functions and Abstraction

The next program does almost the same thing as the previous one, but it declares and calls a function named "displayMessage()" to create and initialize the "p" DOM element, rather than doing it within the greetPerson() function.

The program then makes several more calls to the displayMessage() function, passing a different message each time.

Separating the part of the program that creates and displays the "p" element from the part that builds the message string is an example of "abstraction". Abstraction hides unnecessary details, making it easier to read and understand the program.

Abstraction also saves the programmer time and work by making it unnecessary to re-type the same sequence of statements over and over again to do similar things. Instead, a function can be declared once and called many times, passing in different parameters each time. And if that same sequence of statements ever needs to be changed for any reason, proper abstraction means that it will only need to be changed in one place.

Follow the steps given in previous sections to create and run the program.

```
<html>
<body>
<script type="text/javascript">

        function greetJoe() // This will be called first.
        {
                // Call greetPerson() and pass in "Joe".
                greetPerson("Joe");
        }

        function greetPerson(personName)
        {
                // Call displayMessage() with various arguments
                // to display several different messages.
                displayMessage("Hello, " + personName + "!");
                displayMessage("No time to talk right now.");
                displayMessage("I have to do this thing.");
                displayMessage("It's not just an excuse.");
                displayMessage("See you later...");
        }

        function displayMessage(message)
        {
                // Create p element, set its content, add to page.
                var pGreeting = document.createElement("p");
                pGreeting.innerHTML = message;
                document.body.appendChild(pGreeting);
        }

        // Call greetJoe(), which calls greetPerson(),
        // which calls displayMessage() several times.
        greetJoe();

</script>
</body>
</html>
```

User Input and User Interfaces

All the programs so far have run without asking the user to provide any information.

For example, some of the preceding programs displayed the message, "Hello, Joe!", despite the fact that the user's name is probably not Joe. A more useful program might ask the user what their name is before greeting them by that name. Information provided by the user is called "user input".

The next program displays a "user interface", or "UI", made up of a label, a text box, and a button. (These and other elements of a user interface are called "controls".) When the user enters his or her name into the text box and clicks the button, a personalized greeting is displayed.

The program also includes an "event handler". Event handlers are functions that are called automatically whenever the user interacts with a control in the UI in a certain way. In this program, the event handler is named "buttonGreetClicked", and it is assigned to the button's "onclick" event, which means it is called automatically whenever the user clicks the button.

Inside the handler, there is a call to "document.getElementById()", which returns a "handle" to the DOM element whose ID matches the specified string. This handle can be stored in a variable and used to access the properties of the control, for example, the text string that the user entered into a text box.

Follow the steps given in previous sections to create and run the program.

```
<html>
<body>
<script type="text/javascript">

        // Create a label, text box, and button.
        var labelPersonName = document.createElement("label");
        labelPersonName.innerHTML = "Name of Person to Greet:";
        document.body.appendChild(labelPersonName);

        var inputPerson = document.createElement("input");
        inputPerson.id = "inputPerson";
        document.body.appendChild(inputPerson);

        var buttonGreet = document.createElement("button");
        buttonGreet.innerHTML = "Greet";
        buttonGreet.onclick = buttonGreetClicked; // event handler
        document.body.appendChild(buttonGreet);

        // This function's a "handler" for the button's click event.
        function buttonGreetClicked()
        {
                var inputPerson;
                inputPerson = document.getElementById("inputPerson");
                var personName = inputPerson.value;
                greetPerson(personName);
        }

        function greetPerson(personName) // Build + display greeting.
        {
                var pGreeting = document.createElement("p");
                pGreeting.innerHTML = "Hello, " + personName + "!";
                document.body.appendChild(pGreeting);
        }

</script>
</body>
</html>
```

HTML User Interfaces

The next program does the same thing as the preceding one, but instead of declaring the controls that make up the user interface in the JavaScript program, it instead declares them in the HTML of the web page that contains the program, just before the program itself. Creating a user interface in this way can often be faster and easier to write and to read.

This program also contains a comment in the HTML, rather than in the JavaScript. The comment looks like this:

```
<!-- user interface -->
```

This is basically the same as a JavaScript comment, in that it doesn't really do anything. But it must be formatted differently because it appears outside the "script" element.

Follow the steps given in previous sections to create and run the program. Note that no code will actually execute until the user clicks the "Greet" button.

```
<html>
<body>

<!-- user interface -->

<!-- It's faster to create the controls up here, -->
<!-- rather than in the JavaScript itself. -->
<label>Name of Person to Greet:</label>
<input id="inputPerson"></input>
<button onclick="buttonGreetClicked();">Greet</button>

<script type="text/javascript">

        function buttonGreetClicked()
        {
                // Get the text box from the page.
                var inputPerson = document.getElementById
                (
                    "inputPerson"
                );

                // Assign the contents of the text box to a variable.
                var personName = inputPerson.value;

                // Display a personalized greeting.
                greetPerson(personName);
        }

        function greetPerson(personName)
        {
                var message = "Hello, " + personName + "!";
                alert(message);
        }

</script>
</body>
</html>
```

More User Interfaces

The next program's user interface allows the user to input numbers into a pair of text boxes, choose one of four arithmetic operations (add, subtract, multiply, or divide) from a select box, then click a button to calculate and display the result.

The program makes use of a wider variety of controls than any of the previous programs. It uses three "input" (text box) elements. Two of these inputs are used to accept input from the user. The other is used to display the output, and cannot be modified by the user directly. There is also a "select" element that contains several child "option" elements. The select element is rendered as a "drop-down box" that allows the user to choose between one of the four arithmetic operations supported.

This program makes use of JavaScript's built-in "parseFloat()" function, which takes a string representation of a number as its argument and returns the corresponding numeric value. For example, if this function is passed the string value "123", it will return the numeric value 123.

Follow the steps given in previous sections to create and run the program.

```
<html>
<body>

<!-- user interface -->

<input id="inputOperand0" type="number"]></input>
<select id="selectOperation">
        <option>+</option>
        <option>-</option>
        <option>*</option>
        <option>/</option>
</select>
<input id="inputOperand1" type="number"></input>
<button onclick="buttonEqualsClicked();">=</button>
<input id="inputResult" readOnly="true" value="[Result]"></input>

<script type="text/javascript">

        function buttonEqualsClicked() // Runs when button clicked.
        {
                // Get the text boxes from the page by ID.
                var inputOperand0 = document.getElementById
                (
                        "inputOperand0"
                );
                var inputOperand1 = document.getElementById
                (
                        "inputOperand1"
                );

                // Get strings from text boxes, convert to numbers.
                var operand0AsText = inputOperand0.value;
                var operand1AsText = inputOperand1.value;
                var operand0 = parseFloat(operand0AsText);
                var operand1 = parseFloat(operand1AsText);

                // Determine which operation was specified.
                var selectOperation = document.getElementById
                (
                        "selectOperation"
                );
```

65

```
        var optionOperation =
                selectOperation.selectedOptions[0];
        var operation = optionOperation.value;

        // Do operation on operands and store result.
        var result;
        if (operation == "+")
        {
                result = operand0 + operand1;
        }
        else if (operation == "-")
        {
                result = operand0 - operand1;
        }
        else if (operation == "*")
        {
                result = operand0 * operand1;
        }
        else if (operation == "/")
        {
                result = operand0 / operand1;
        }
        else
        {
                result = "Error!";
        }

        // Display the result on the page.
        var inputResult;
        inputResult = document.getElementById("inputResult");
        inputResult.value = result;
}

</script>
</body>
</html>
```

(This page intentionally left blank to preserve section format.)

Data Structures, Classes, and Objects

Previously, variables have been assigned several different kinds of values. Each of these "kinds" of values are called a "data type", or just a "type". The data types we have seen so far are strings, numbers and "booleans" (true-false values). These simple data types are called "primitives".

Some kinds of data, however, are more complicated than just a simple number or string of text. In these cases, it is helpful for the programmer to be able to create new, more complex data types, called "data structures" or "classes".

As an example, consider a mailing address. In the United States, mailing addresses are made up of the name of the addressee, the street that the addressee lives on, the city and state that he or she lives in, and a postal (ZIP) code.

One way to store an address might simply be to put all that information in a single string, for example, "Joe Blow, 123 Fake Street, Nowheresville, WY, 81009" . But storing an address this way makes it difficult to access the individual parts of the address later. If the programmer wanted to, say, loop through an array of addresses to find just the ones located in the state of Idaho, it would be necessary to break each address string into substrings and then find the particular substring that corresponds to the state before seeing if it matches the desired value. All this processing is a lot of work.

One solution to this problem might be to use a different variable for each of the individual parts of the address. For example, instead of a single string variable named "address", one might instead see several variables, perhaps named "addressName", "addressStreet", "addressCity", "addressState", and "addressZIP". But using so many variables to represent a single address makes things difficult in other ways. To revisit to the programming problem described in the previous paragraph, what would happen if the programmer needed to create an array of addresses? Should there be a separate array for each individual type of data, for example, an array of names, an array of streets, an array of cities, an array of states, and an array of ZIP codes? It is easy to seee that such a solution would quickly become unwieldly and inconvenient.

To solve these problems, the next program declares a "class" named "Address" to hold all of the various pieces of information for a particular address in one convenient structure. It then creates three new "instances" of this class, each of which represents a different person's address. Each of these "objects" is assigned to a different variable. The addressee's name, street, city, state, and postal code will be accessible as "members" or "fields" on a particular Address object.

In JavaScript, a class is declared as a special kind a function, called a "constructor". The fields of the class will typically be passed in the argument list of the function header. Inside the body of the constructor function, the values of these arguments will be assigned to the fields of the class, using the "this" keyword. The whole class declaration looks like this:

```
function Address(addressee, street, city, state, zip)
{
        this.addressee = addressee;
        this.street = street;
        this.city = city;
        this.state = state;
        this.zip = zip;
}
```

To create a new address "instance" or "object" based on the Address class, the program uses the "new" keyword, followed by "Address", followed by the values of all the fields in the class in the same order as in the function header, like this:

```
var joesAddress = new Address
(
        "Joe Blow",
        "123 Fake Street",
        "Nowheresville", "WY", "81009"
```

```
    );
```

Once an object has been created, a particular field of that object can be accessed in code by appending a dot ("".") to the name of the variable that contains the data structure, followed by the name of the field, like this:

```
var theCityWhereJoeLives = joesAddress.city;
```

The next program creates an array of objects, each of which is an instance of the class named "Address", and then calls a function to display each of them to the screen.

Follow the steps given in previous sections to create and run the program.

```html
<html>
<body>
<script type="text/javascript">

        function displayTwoAddresses()
        {
                // Create an Address object.
                var address0 = new Address
                (
                        "Alan West",
                        "1145 Batpole Lane",
                        "Gotham", "NY", "12345"
                );

                // Create another Address object.
                var address1 = new Address
                (
                        "Jenny Igotchanumba",
                        "1982 Tutone Terrace",
                        "Tutown", "DE", "75309"
                );

                // Put the addresses in an array.
                var addresses = [address0, address1];

                // Loop through the address array.
                for (var i = 0; i < addresses.length; i++)
                {
                        var address = addresses[i];
                        displayAddress(address);
                }
        } // End of displayTwoAddresses() function declaration.

        // This is the beginning of the Address class.
        function Address(addressee, street, city, state, zip)
        {
                // This is the "constructor" of the Address class.

                // Set the "fields" of the Address object
                // with the corresponding arguments.
                this.addressee = addressee;
```

71

```
            this.street = street;
            this.city = city;
            this.state = state;
            this.zip = zip;
    } // This is the end of the constructor.
    // This is the end of the Address class.

    function displayAddress(address)
    {
            var newline = "<br />";

            // Concatenate the fields of the Address object
            // into a single string.
            var addressAsString =
                    address.addressee + newline
                    + address.street + newline
                    + address.city + " "
                    + address.state + " "
                    + address.zip + newline;

            // Display the string.
            var divAddress = document.createElement("div");
            divAddress.innerHTML = addressAsString;
            document.body.appendChild(divAddress);
    }

    // Call the displayTwoAddresses() function.
    displayTwoAddresses();

</script>
</body>
</html>
```

(This page intentionally left blank to preserve section format.)

Class Prototypes and Methods

The next program does the same thing as the preceding one, but it replaces the function named "displayAddress()" with an equivalent function named "display()" that is associated with the "prototype" of the Address class. A function associated with a particular class in this way is called a "method" of that class.

Within a method, the "this" keyword can be used to access the class's fields, just like in its constructor.

In the previous program, the call to the display function was made like this:

```
displayAddress(address);
```

In this program, an equivalent call can be made like this:

```
address.display();
```

Grouping the functions that operate on a data structure with the data structure itself is an example of an idea called "encapsulation". Proper encapsulation makes it easier to write, read and understand a program.

Follow the steps given in previous sections to create and run the program.

```
<html>
<body>
<script type="text/javascript">

        function displayTwoAddresses()
        {
                // Create an Address object.
                var address0 = new Address
                (
                        "Alan West",
                        "1145 Batpole Lane",
                        "Gotham", "NY", "12345"
                );

                // Create another Address object.
                var address1 = new Address
                (
                        "Jenny Igotchanumba",
                        "1982 Tutone Terrace",
                        "Tutown", "DE", "75309"
                );

                // Put the addresses in an array.
                var addresses = [address0, address1];

                // Loop through the address array.
                for (var i = 0; i < addresses.length; i++)
                {
                        var address = addresses[i];
                        // Call the Address object's display() method.
                        address.display();
                }
        } // End of displayTwoAddresses() function declaration.

        // This is the start of the Address class.
        function Address(addressee, street, city, state, zip)
        {
                // This is the constructor of the Address class.

                this.addressee = addressee;
                this.street = street;
```

```
                    this.city = city;
                    this.state = state;
                    this.zip = zip;

                    // This is the end of the Address constructor.
            }
            {

                    // Below is the sole method of the Address class.

                    Address.prototype.display = function()
                    {
                            var newline = "<br />";

                            var addressAsString =
                                    this.addressee + newline
                                    + this.street + newline
                                    + this.city + " "
                                    + this.state + " "
                                    + this.zip + newline;

                            var divAddress = document.createElement("div");
                            divAddress.innerHTML = addressAsString;
                            document.body.appendChild
                            (
                                    divAddress
                            );
                    }

            } // This is the end of the Address class.

            // Call the displayTwoAddresses() function.
            displayTwoAddresses();

    </script>
    </body>
    </html>
```

(This page intentionally left blank to preserve section format.)

Objects as Function Arguments

The next program shows how objects are handled differently than primitives when being passed as arguments to a function.

When primitive values, such as strings and numbers, are passed as arguments to a function, the function is given a copy of the values to work with. Any changes the function makes to a primitive argument's value are only effective within that function itself. When the function finishes running and control returns to the main program, the primitive variable that was passed as an argument still retains its original value from before it was passed into the function call, regardless of how that argument might have been modified inside the function.

When, on the other hand, an object is passed as an argument to a function, the function receives a reference to that object, rather than a copy of it. This means that any changes made to the fields of that object within the function are permanent, and remain in place even after the function finishes executing.

Primitives, then, are said to be "passed by value", while objects are said to be "passed by reference". This is a common source of confusion and frustration to beginning programmers. The reasons for this are too complicated to explain fully here, but they have to do with how the different data types are stored in the JavaScript's "memory". Variables of object data types are actually "pointers", which are essentially addresses of the location in memory the actual object data is stored, while variables of primitive data types contain the actual values themselves.

Follow the steps given in previous sections to create and run the program.

```
<html>
<body>
<script type="text/javascript">

        // First we double a primitive using a function...

        function doubleNumberPrimitive(numberToDouble)
        {
                numberToDouble = 2 * numberToDouble;
        }

        var numberPrimitive = 42;
        alert("numberPrimitive before is " + numberPrimitive);
        doubleNumberPrimitive(numberPrimitive);
        alert("numberPrimitive after is " + numberPrimitive);

        // ...then we double a field on an object using a function.

        function NumberObject(value)
        {
                this.value = value;
        }

        function doubleNumberObject(numberObjectToDouble)
        {
                numberObjectToDouble.value =
                        2 * numberObjectToDouble.value;
        }

        var numberObject = new NumberObject(42);
        alert("numberObject.value before is " + numberObject.value);
        doubleNumberObject(numberObject);
        alert("numberObject.value after is " + numberObject.value);

</script>
</body>
</html>
```

Graphics

The next program creates a "canvas" DOM element, creates a "graphics context" for that canvas, and then calls various functions on the graphics context object to draw some text and several shapes, including a rectangle, a triangle, and a circle, to the canvas element.

Follow the steps given in previous sections to create and run the program. Then try changing some of the numbers and colors and run the program again to see what happens.

```
<html>
<body>
<script type="text/javascript">

        var canvas = document.createElement("canvas");
        canvas.width = 100;
        canvas.height= 100;
        document.body.appendChild(canvas);

        var graphics = canvas.getContext("2d");

        graphics.strokeStyle = "Black";
        graphics.strokeRect(0, 0, 100, 100); // Black box.

        graphics.fillStyle = "Red";
        graphics.fillRect(10, 20, 30, 40); // Solid red rectangle.

        graphics.strokeStyle = "Green";
        graphics.beginPath();
        graphics.arc(80, 20, 10, 0, Math.PI * 2);
        graphics.stroke(); // Green circle at (80, 20), radius 10.

        graphics.beginPath();
        graphics.moveTo(50, 50);
        graphics.lineTo(90, 50);
        graphics.lineTo(70, 70);
        graphics.closePath();
        graphics.fillStyle = "Blue";
        graphics.fill(); // Blue triangle...
        graphics.strokeStyle = "Orange";
        graphics.lineWidth = 5;
        graphics.stroke(); // ...with orange border.

        graphics.fillStyle = "Violet";
        graphics.fillText("texty text text", 10, 90); // Purple text.

</script>
</body>
</html>
```

Timers

The next program displays a couple of buttons named "Start" and "Stop".

When "Start" button is clicked, the current date and time is displayed, and that display is updated once per second. To do this, it calls the "setInterval()" function, which, just like the "alert()" function, is built into JavaScript. The setInterval() function takes two arguments. The first argument is a function to be called at regular time intervals, and the second is the length of that interval in milliseconds. For example, to call a function named "doAThing()" once every second, the following code would be used:

```
var doAThingEachSecond = setInterval(doAThing, 1000);
```

A timer that has been started with the setInterval() function can be stopped by passing it in as an argument to the clearInterval() function, as shown below:

```
clearInterval(doAThingEachSecond);
```

In this program, the clearInterval() function is called when the user clicks the "Stop" button.

The startInterval() function can be used to create "real-time" programs that automatically update their output every few seconds or even every few milliseconds.

```html
<html>
<body>
<p id="pTime">[Current Time]</p>
<button id="buttonStart" onclick="startTimer();">Start</button>
<button id="buttonStop" onclick="stopTimer();">Stop</button>
<script type="text/javascript">

        var timer = null;

        function startTimer()
        {
                // Call displayTime() each second.
                var millisecondsPerTimerTick = 1000;
                timer = setInterval
                (
                        displayTime, millisecondsPerTimerTick
                );
                displayTime(); // Display immediately.
        }

        function stopTimer()
        {
                clearInterval(timer); // Stop the timer.
        }

        function displayTime()
        {
                // Create a new Date object,
                // which contains the current time by default.
                var timeCurrent = new Date();

                var pTime = document.getElementById("pTime");
                pTime.innerHTML = timeCurrent;
        }

</script>
</body>
</html>
```

Animation

The next program combines graphics and a timer to display a simple animation.

An animation consists of a series of still images, or "frames", which are displayed in rapid succession to create the illusion of motion. The animation in this program contains ten frames, one of which is displayed every 25 milliseconds, when the timer automatically calls the drawAnimationFrame() function over and over again.

Each time drawAnimationFrame() is called, it increments the current frame number, calculates the fraction of the current cycle remaining, and uses that information to redraw the foreground object slightly differently each frame. After the last frame in the sequence is displayed, the current frame number is set back to 0, so the animation loops back to the first frame and starts over. Since a full cycle of ten frames takes a total of 250 milliseconds, the animation will repeat four times every second.

```html
<html>
<body>
<canvas id="canvasToDrawTo" width="100" height="100"></canvas>
<script type="text/javascript">

        // Get canvas from the page, get graphics context for it.
        var canvas = document.getElementById("canvasToDrawTo");
        var graphics = canvas.getContext("2d");

        var framesPerCycle = 10; // Repeat after 10 frames.
        var frameCurrent = 0; // Start on the first frame.
        var mouthAngleMax = Math.PI / 4;
        // Call drawAnimationFrame() every 25 milliseconds.
        setInterval(drawAnimationFrame, 25);

        function drawAnimationFrame()
        {
                // Blank out the background.
                graphics.fillStyle = "Black";
                graphics.fillRect(0, 0, 100, 100);

                frameCurrent++; // Next frame
                if (frameCurrent >= framesPerCycle)
                {
                        // Cycle complete; return to the first frame.
                        frameCurrent = 0;
                }
                var fractionOfCycleDone = frameCurrent / framesPerCycle;
                var fractionOfCycleLeft = 1 - fractionOfCycleDone;
                var mouthAngle = fractionOfCycleLeft * mouthAngleMax;

                // Draw the foreground object.
                graphics.fillStyle = "Yellow";
                graphics.beginPath();
                graphics.moveTo(50, 50);
                graphics.arc
                (
                        50, 50, // center
                        30, // radius
                        mouthAngle, // start angle
```

85

```
                Math.PI * 2 - mouthAngle // stop angle
        );
        graphics.closePath();
        graphics.fill();
    }

</script>
</body>
</html>
```

(This page intentionally left blank to preserve section format.)

Keyboard Input

The previous programs either ignore user input, or accept it only through controls like text boxes and buttons. While this is of course useful in many applications, it is not helpful when instant responses to user actions are required, as in most video games. In such situations, other methods are used to monitor user input. For the keyboard, this may be done by assigning an event handler to the "keydown" event of the document.body object, like this:

```
document.body.onkeydown = handleEventKeydown;

function handleEventKeydown(keyEvent)
{
        var nameOfKeyPressed = keyEvent.key;
        alert("nameOfKeyPressed is " + nameOfKeyPressed);
}
```

Once a function is assigned as the handler of the "keydown" event, JavaScript will called it automatically each time the user presses a key. The argument of the keydown event handler, named "keyEvent" in the example above, is an instance of a class named "Keyboard-Event", which is is built into JavaScript. JavaScript creates new a KeyboardEvent object for each keypress, which is then passed in the call to the handler function. Each KeyboardEvent object has fields that describe what key was pressed, along with other information like whether the Shift or Control keys were being held down as well.

In the next program, a function named handleEventKeydown() is assigned as the handler of document.body's "keydown" event. Each time a key is pressed, the name of that key is displayed.

Follow the usual steps to create and run the program.

```
<html>
<body>
<script type="text/javascript">

        function startGettingKeyboardInput()
        {
                // Create p element, set its id, add it to page.
                var pKeyPressed = document.createElement("p");
                pKeyPressed.id = "pKeyPressed";
                document.body.appendChild(pKeyPressed);

                // Assign the handleEventKeydown() function
                // as the handler for document.body's keydown event.
                document.body.onkeydown = handleEventKeydown;
        }

        function handleEventKeydown(keydownEvent)
        {
                // Get the name of the key pressed.
                var nameOfKeyPressed = keydownEvent.key;

                // Get the p element from page, set its content.
                var pKeyPressed = document.getElementById
                (
                        "pKeyPressed"
                );
                pKeyPressed.innerHTML =
                        "Key Pressed: " + nameOfKeyPressed;
        }

        startGettingKeyboardInput();

</script>
</body>
</html>
```

Mouse Input

Just as keyboard input can be monitored by assigning a handler function to the "keydown" event of the document.body object, so can mouse input be monitored by assigning a handler function to document.body's "mousedown" event.

For the mousedown event, however, the MouseEvent class takes the place of the KeyboardEvent. Every time the mouse is clicked on the page, JavaScript builds a new instance of the MouseEvent class and passes it as the argument of a call to the assigned mousedown handler function.

Within the handler function, the fields of the MouseEvent argument can be accessed to provide information about the mouse click, such as which of the mouse's buttons was clicked and the the coordinates of the mouse cursor at the time.

The next program assigns an event handler to document.body's mousedown event to to display the position of any mouse clicks made by the user on the page. It should be noted that, in order for the mouse click to be detected by the program, the mouse cursor must be hovering somewhere over the web page when the button is clicked.

Follow the usual steps to create and run the program.

```
<html>
<body>
<script type="text/javascript">

        function startGettingMouseInput()
        {
                // Create p element, set its ID, add it to page.
                var pMouseClickPos = document.createElement("p");
                pMouseClickPos.id = "pMouseClickPos";
                document.body.appendChild(pMouseClickPos);

                // Assign the handleEventMousedown() function
                // as the handler of document.body's mousedown event.
                document.body.onmousedown = handleEventMousedown;
        }

        function handleEventMousedown(mouseEvent)
        {
                // Get the p element from the page.
                var pMouseClickPos = document.getElementById
                (
                        "pMouseClickPos"
                );

                // Set the p element's content
                // based on the position of the mouse click.
                pMouseClickPos.innerHTML =
                        "Mouse clicked at: ("
                        + event.x + "," + event.y
                        + ")";
        }

        startGettingMouseInput();

</script>
</body>
</html>
```

91

A Simple Game

The next program is a very simple game. It combines graphics, a timer, and keyboard input to allow the user to move a rectangle slowly around the screen. The goal is to touch the green circle with the gray circle. It's not very exciting, but it does illustrate the main concepts of game programming.

This program makes use of the "bind()" function built in to JavaScript to assign the event handlers for the keyboard inputs and the timer ticks. This is done so that the "this" keyword in those event handler functions can be used to access the fields on the Game object. Without the bind() function, any references to "this" in the handler functions would not correspond to to the Game object as desired, but rather to an object called "window", which represents the web browser's main window.

Follow the usual steps to create and run the program. Use the arrow keys to move the gray circle around, and try to touch the green circle.

```
<html>
<body>
<script type="text/javascript">

function main()
{
        new Game();
}

// Class declarations start here.

function Game()
{
        var players =
        [
                new Player
                (
                        "LightGray",
                        4, // radius
                        new Coords(10, 10), // pos
                        true // isUser
                ),
                new Player
                (
                        "Green",
                        4, // radius
                        new Coords(50, 50), // pos
                        false // isUser
                ),
        ];

        this.world = new World
        (
                "White",
                new Coords(100, 100), // size
                players
        );

        // Create a canvas element and add it to the page.
        var canvas = document.createElement("canvas");
        canvas.width = this.world.size.x;
```

```
        canvas.height = this.world.size.y;
        document.body.appendChild(canvas);

        // Get a graphics context for the canvas.
        this.graphics = canvas.getContext("2d");

        // Assign keyboard event handler functions.
        document.body.onkeydown = this.handleEventKeyDown.bind
        (
                this
        );
        document.body.onkeyup = this.handleEventKeyUp.bind
        (
                this
        );

        // Start the timer.
        this.timer = setInterval
        (
                this.updateForTimerTick.bind(this),
                100 // millisecondsPerTimerTick
        );
}
{

        Game.prototype.handleEventKeyDown = function(event)
        {
                this.keyPressed = event.key;
        }

        Game.prototype.handleEventKeyUp = function(event)
        {
                this.keyPressed = null;
        }

        Game.prototype.updateForTimerTick = function()
        {
                this.world.draw(this.graphics);

                this.world.updateForTimerTick(this.keyPressed);

                var doPlayersCollide =
```

```
                    this.world.doPlayersCollide();

            if (doPlayersCollide == true)
            {
                    clearInterval(this.timer);
                    alert("You win!")
            }
    }
}

function Coords(x, y)
{
        // Coordinates on the XY plane,
        // such as a position or size.
        this.x = x;
        this.y = y;
}
{
        Coords.prototype.add = function(other)
        {
                // Add coordinates to another.
                this.x += other.x;
                this.y += other.y;
                return this;
        }

        Coords.prototype.clone = function()
        {
                // Create a new Coords object
                // with identical x and y values.
                return new Coords(this.x, this.y);
        }

        Coords.prototype.magnitude = function()
        {
                // How far are these coordinates
                // from the origin at (0, 0)?
                return Math.sqrt
                (
                    this.x * this.x
                      + this.y * this.y
```

```
                );
        }

        Coords.prototype.subtract = function(other)
        {
                // Subtract coordinates from another.
                this.x -= other.x;
                this.y -= other.y;
                return this;
        }
}

function Player(color, radius, pos, isUser)
{
        this.color = color;
        this.radius = radius;
        this.pos = pos;
        this.isUser = isUser;
}
{
        // static variables
        Player.Directions =
        [
                new Coords(1, 0),
                new Coords(-1, 0),
                new Coords(0, 1),
                new Coords(0, -1),
        ];

        // instance methods
        Player.prototype.draw = function(graphics)
        {
                // Use the graphics context passed in
                // to draw a circle of this players color.
                graphics.fillStyle = this.color;
                graphics.beginPath();
                graphics.arc
                (
                        this.pos.x,
                        this.pos.y,
                        this.radius,
```

```
                0, Math.PI * 2
        );
        graphics.fill();
}

Player.prototype.move = function(keyPressed)
{
        var directions = Player.Directions;
        var directionToMove;
        if (this.isUser == false)
        {
                // Player is computer-controlled
                // rather than by the user:
                // pick a random direction.
                var dirIndex = Math.floor
                (
                        Math.random()
                        * directions.length
                );

                directionToMove = directions[dirIndex];
        }
        // Else player is controlled by user,
        // so check keys to see which direction
        // the user wants to move.
        else if (keyPressed == "ArrowDown") // down
        {
                directionToMove = directions[2];
        }
        else if (keyPressed == "ArrowLeft") // left
        {
                directionToMove = directions[1];
        }
        else if (keyPressed == "ArrowRight") // right
        {
                directionToMove = directions[0];
        }
        else if (keyPressed == "ArrowUp") // up
        {
                directionToMove = directions[3];
        }
```

```
            else
            {
                    // If no arrow key is pressed,
                    // dont move at all.
                    directionToMove = new Coords(0, 0);
            }

            this.pos.add(directionToMove);
    }
}


function World(color, size, players)
{
        this.color = color;
        this.size = size;
        this.players = players;
}
{
        World.prototype.updateForTimerTick = function(keyPressed)
        {
                for (var i = 0; i < this.players.length; i++)
                {
                        var player = this.players[i];
                        player.move(keyPressed);
                }
        }

        World.prototype.doPlayersCollide = function()
        {
                var player1 = this.players[1];
                var player1Pos = player1.pos.clone();
                var distanceOfPlayers = player1Pos.subtract
                (
                        this.players[0].pos
                ).magnitude();

                var sumOfPlayerRadii =
                        this.players[0].radius
                        + this.players[1].radius;

                var doPlayersCollide =
```

```
                    (distanceOfPlayers < sumOfPlayerRadii);

            return doPlayersCollide;
        }

        World.prototype.draw = function(graphics)
        {
            // Draw the background.
            graphics.fillStyle = this.color;
            graphics.fillRect
            (
                    0, 0,
                    this.size.x,
                    this.size.y
            );

            // Draw the border.
            graphics.strokeStyle = "Gray";
            graphics.strokeRect
            (
                    0, 0,
                    this.size.x,
                    this.size.y
            );

            // Draw the players.
            for (var i = 0; i < this.players.length; i++)
            {
                    var player = this.players[i];
                    player.draw(graphics);
            }
        }
}

main();

</script>
</body>
</html>
```

Part III

Conclusion

Moving Forward

You now know how to write simple programs in JavaScript. But there's always more to learn.

There are whole libraries of information out there to teach you more about programming. There are tons of resources out there about writing incredibly useful business software, creating mind-blowing graphics and animations, passing secret messages back and forth, or even something as simple as sorting a list in the fastest way possible.

There are many more programming languages out there besides JavaScript, too. There's C, C++ (pronounced "cee-plus-plus"), and Java, which are very popular languages that allow faster and more powerful programs to be written that run outside the web browser. There's assembly language, which is a very "low-level" language that the main microchip in your computer (the "processor") understands. There's BASIC and Pascal, which historically have been used to teach beginners to program for decades. There are relatively new languages like Python and Ruby that are being learned by more and more programmers every day. There are more specialized languages like SQL, LISP, and LOGO that are designed to efficiently store and access trillions of bytes of data or to solve complex math problems or even draw intricate designs. And there are hundreds of other languages out there, with more being added to the list every year.

The possibilities are endless. Have fun!

www.ingramcontent.com/pod-product-compliance
Lightning Source LLC
Chambersburg PA
CBHW022104170526
45157CB00004B/1479